QUAIL SONG

A Pueblo Indian Tale adapted by **Valerie Scho Carey**

illustrated by **Ivan Barnett**

A WHITEBIRD BOOK

G. P. Putnam's Sons

New York

G. P. Putnam's Sons, a division of The Putnam & Grosset Book Group,
200 Madison Avenue, New York, NY 10016
Published simultaneously in Canada
Printed in Hong Kong by South China Printing Co. (1988) Ltd.
Type design by Gunta Alexander

Library of Congress Cataloging-in-Publication Data
Carey, Valerie Scho. Quail song: a Pueblo Indian tale/by Valerie Scho Carey;
illustrated by Ivan Barnett. p.cm. "A Whitebird book." Summary: A
retelling of a traditional Pueblo Indian tale in which Quail outwits a
persistent Coyote. 1. Pueblo Indians—Legends. 2. Indians of North
America—Southwest, New—Legends. [1. Pueblo Indians—Legends.
2. Indians of North America—Southwest, New—Legends.] I. Barnett,
Ivan, ill. II. Title. E99.P9C27 1990   398.2′08997—dc19 [E]
89-3872 CIP AC   ISBN 0-399-21936-6
1 3 5 7 9 10 8 6 4 2
First impression

For Brent, Kimberly, Allison and Jeffrey,
with love — VSC

For my father, Isa, with love — IB

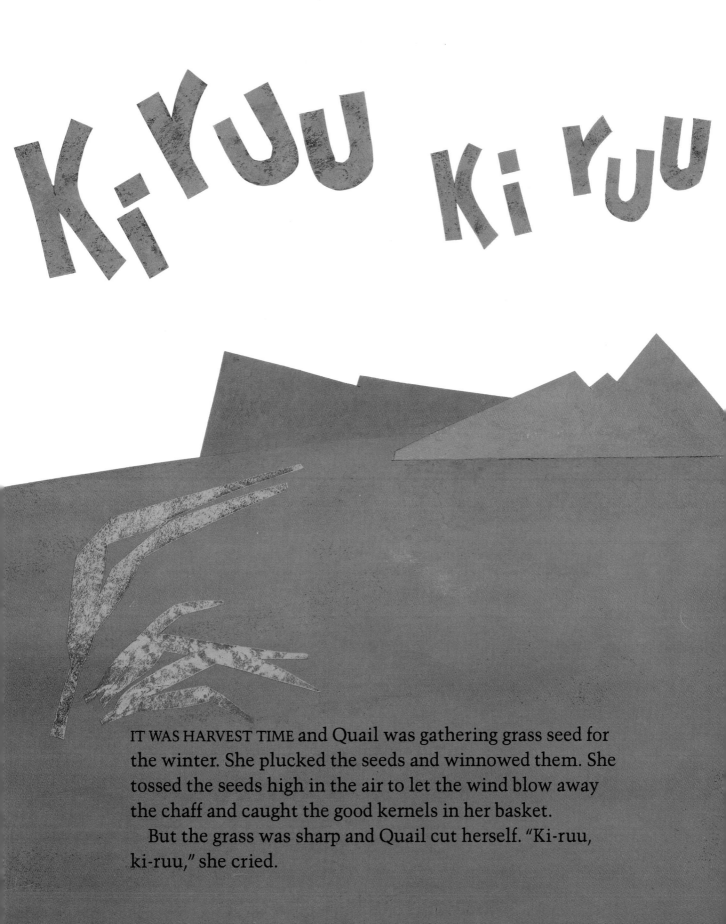

KI-RUU KI RUU

IT WAS HARVEST TIME and Quail was gathering grass seed for the winter. She plucked the seeds and winnowed them. She tossed the seeds high in the air to let the wind blow away the chaff and caught the good kernels in her basket.

But the grass was sharp and Quail cut herself. "Ki-ruu, ki-ruu," she cried.

ruu ki ruu

Coyote was walking by and heard Quail crying "ki-ruu, ki-ruu." "What a beautiful song," he said to himself. "It would make a pretty lullaby for my little ones. I must find whoever is singing and tell them to teach it to me."

Coyote followed the song into the grass and found Quail hopping on one foot as though doing a little dance and moaning "ki-ruu, ki-ruu."

"Quail, teach me your song," Coyote demanded. "I must have it to sing my little ones to sleep."

"I was not singing," Quail answered. "I was winnowing when I cut myself on the sharp grass. See?" she said, holding out her little foot and fanning it pfft, pfft to show Coyote where the cut still hurt.

"Pooh!" said Coyote. "Do you think I am such a fool that I cannot tell singing from crying? Now teach me your song or I shall swallow you up."

Poor Quail did not wish to be swallowed up, so she
taught Coyote to cry as she had.

"Ki-ruu, ki-ruu," sang Coyote. "I must take this song to
my little ones."

Coyote hastened off leaving Quail to return to her winnowing. But as Coyote ran along he tripped in a prairie-dog hole and dropped his precious song. "Ki, ki," he squeaked, for that was all he could remember of it. "I must go back to Quail and tell her to teach me the song again."

So Coyote went back and found Quail still winnowing the grass seed and he said to her, "Quail, I tripped in a prairie-dog hole and dropped the song. You must sing it for me again so that I can carry it home to my little ones."

"But I have told you before," protested Quail, "I was not singing. I was crying."

Coyote snarled and showed his teeth to Quail. "If you do not sing for me, I will swallow you up like this! SNAP! SNAP!" And Coyote snapped his mouth open and shut so that Quail could feel his hot breath and smell the sour smell of his insides.

"Ki-ruu, ki-ruu," cried Quail, for she did not wish to be eaten up.

"Thank you," said Coyote. "I will hold on tighter to the song this time." And he sprang away into the tall grass.

Coyote was so happy to have the song again that he did not look where he was going and he trod on a rattlesnake's tail. Now Coyote was quick and he jumped clear of the snake's angry bite, but in so doing he dropped the song.

Once more, all he could remember was "ki, ki." "That," Coyote fretted, "would not sing anyone to sleep. I must go back to Quail and tell her to teach me her song again."

Coyote found Quail still winnowing. "Quail, a snake tried to bite me. I had to twist and jump to get out of the way of his fangs and in so doing I dropped the song. Now sing it for me again so that I can carry it home to my little ones."

Again Quail protested, "I was not singing. I was crying."

Again Coyote snarled fiercely and said, "If you do not sing
for me, I will SWALLOW YOU UP!"

So Quail cried, "Ki-ruu, ki-ruu."

"Thank you," said Coyote, "I know I will hold on tightly
this time." And off he went singing happily to himself,
"Ki-ruu, ki-ruu."

When Coyote left, Quail said to herself, "It seems I am to get little work done here. Every time I begin, that foolish Coyote comes back. I would be wise to leave this place before he grows tired of this-song-that-is-no-song and gobbles me up."

So Quail painted eyes on a rock that was just her size and left a small basket of seeds nearby so that if Coyote were to come again he would think Quail was still there and he would not go looking for her. "Let him try to get a song out of that one," said Quail and she went away.

As Coyote drew nearer home, he ran faster and faster. He darted and leapt across the ground, seeming to fly as he went. When he came to a dry gully, he sprang across. But he startled a pair of mourning doves who had been sitting on the farther side and they flew into his face so that he lost his balance and tumbled to the bottom. "Aiee," cried Coyote, "it is lucky that I did not break all my bones, but I have dropped the song and I must go back to Quail and tell her to sing it to me again."

When Coyote returned to the place where Quail had been winnowing, he found the rock that she had painted. But Coyote did not see that it was only a rock and he spoke to it. "I have lost the song a third time," he said, "so you must sing it for me again."

Nothing happened.

"Did you hear me, Quail? Sing the song again or I will swallow you up," said Coyote.

But still nothing happened.

Coyote's lips curled up to show his teeth. "I will count to four," he growled, "and if you do not sing, I will SWALLOW YOU UP! One. Two. Three. Four!"

The-rock-that-looked-like-Quail was silent.

Coyote's jaws gaped open. He sprang and clamped his teeth down hard on the rock. CRUNCH. The teeth broke out of his mouth. "AIEEE!" wailed Coyote. "AIEEE!"

The sound of Coyote's crying awakened Lizard, who had been dozing in the sun nearby. Lizard slipped through the grass, tsi-ka, tsi-ka, tsi-ka, over to where Coyote stood moaning.

"Good day, friend Coyote," said Lizard. "What a beautiful song you are singing! Won't you please teach it to me?"

Coyote pointed to his broken teeth lying in the dust and wailed to the sky, "AIEEE! Lizard, you are so STUPID, you cannot tell crying from singing!" And angry Coyote pounced on Lizard to swallow him up, but Lizard slipped away, tsi-ka, tsi-ka, tsi-ka, for Coyote could not bite without his teeth.

Much ashamed, Coyote slunk away and hid, for now he had lost his teeth as well as the-song-that-was-no-song he had learned from Quail.